Money Management

Ways to Have a Healthy Financial Life

Meenakshi Narang

Table of Contents

Introduction

Sciences, Languages, and Performing Arts are the usual subjects that were taught to us in school. One thing that is never taught to us is the management of our personal finances. And this plays a big part in our lives that is why we must learn to be able to manage the most important aspect of our maintenance - Money.

There is no doubt that money rules our life. But sadly still many of us don't know how to have full control with our finances. Most often than not, during the times of financial abundance or crises, we are more inclined to lose our financial stability. When this happens it may result in mismanagement of our funds. Also, it is never enough to just earn for a living. It is equally important to know how to manage the finances wisely.

This book will provide you with useful information that you can use when spending and managing your financial resources. This takes away the worry of having to suffer financial setbacks in the future.

You will also know more about the fundamentals of money management that is far different from what we learn from the books and journals on budgeting, accounting or finance.
This book will guide you through the process of managing your long term financial goals as well as

learning to save for the future by having sufficient financial buffers.

Chapter 1 – Becoming Financially Literate

One universal fact is, money is an important aspect of our lives. Thus, its management must be mastered lest our finances would go haywire. Many financially well-to-do individuals lose their wits at the time of selecting some saving or insurance for the lack of their knowledge. They fail to take a judicious decision even concerning simple money matters. While many spends huge amount over vocational and communication skills, the basic financial skills are often ignored.

It is imperative to learn about -
- Banking services and financial services
- Consumer loans
- Credit cards
- Investments & Insurance
- Debt Management & Credit Building

- Retirement plans and
- Income tax management

Importance of Personal Financial Management

Knowing your money helps in staying away from bad debts that tend to make our lives extremely miserable. One biggest reason behind managing money is to keep financial crises at bay and live comfortably. As an old saying goes 'Well managed money would manage you well!" here are some reasons to manage our finances –

Avoiding Financial Pitfalls

Despite the world going electronic in every possible sense, money still needs to be managed and supervised by our own acumen. The modern and electronic world also brings with it stealthily hidden financial pitfalls that must be avoided well in time. Thus, learn to manage your finances right from the beginning.

Preventing Wastage

Managing money brings the high level of awareness, and no one can dupe you of your hard earned money. Get knowledge of your bank accounts, deposits, interest rates to saving many pounds and dollar from getting wasted out of discrepancies.

Avoiding Cheating

Staying aware of the finances and their growth will never allow you to get duped. Know how much interest the bank is charging on your deposits; or how much fee is to be paid for a demand draft ready.

Dodge Penalties

Many public utilities' offices announce the discount on timely payment of their bills that can only be spotted by the aware and vigilant individuals. Sometimes, even ATMs also dispense lesser amount thus making the careless individuals suffer the loss.

Dodge Crises

Keeping a tab on money matters can save a mole becoming a mountain. Keeping a vigil on finances will control spending and wasting, and financial crises can be dodged.

Investing Astutely

Managing personal finances would make you aware of good, better and the best investments that could come your way. Else, you might land up taking a wrong credit card that charges the exorbitant rate of interest. Justifiably, no one can be genuinely concerned about your money except you.

Gauging Financial Goof ups

Monetary calamities can be better handled and resolved if financial reins are in control. Plus crisis can be foreseen and tackled effectively to get saved from many sorts of embarrassments.

Strengthening Credit Rating

Control over personal finances will keep debts at bay, and strong credit status will benefit you. You would be eligible to avail some quick loans, buy on credit, or take a long term home or education loan. In short, you will have sound and vigorous financial health.

Realizing Financial Goals

Your short-term, as well as long-term goals, will be easier to attain with minimal liabilities. This would consequently bring in peace of mind and respectable status in family and social circle.

Averting borrowing

Understandably, well-managed finances are going to take care of your family and loved ones. In case of unforeseen bad times, only saved and managed finances will come to your resort thus saving you from begging, borrowing or stealing.

Fundamentals of Money Management

Money management isn't a Herculean task as it may appear to be. Many people often shirk from knowing their money matters in detail as they have a phantom fear of devoting their free time in dealing with Mathematics. Our day to day finances needs mere careful planning and common sense that we all have in abundance. Ignoring them or shirking from knowing our money matters will cease us from getting financially strong and independent. Concerning our personal finances, we ought to know –

> ➢ About the preparation of our household and personal budget so that we can have controlled and wise spending
> ➢ About the working and basic fundamental of banks and other financial institutions so that their facilities can be availed astutely
> ➢ About the status of our accounts, deposits, funds, etc. and what interest the bank given over our deposits

➢ About ensuring online security of funds and finances lest they may get misused or breached
➢ About timely filing and paying of various taxes lest they may invite fines or penalties
➢ About managing and maintaining of financial document for their clarity and validity

Chapter 2 - Appraise Your Current Financial Status

Now since you have decided to learn to manage your personal finances, let us start by appraising your current financial status. There are few questions you must ask yourself to know the equilibrium of your income and expenditure. Answer the following questions –

- Do you often encounter paucity of money for your daily expenses?
- Do you eat frequently out, thus spending a lot of money?
- Do you live paycheck to paycheck?
- Are you at the loss of words when asked how much is your household/personal expenses?

- Do you despise or dread sudden domestic expenditure?
- Have you ever planned your monthly budget?
- Do you save money for a longer or shorter perspective?

If there are more than 4 No as the answer to this questionnaire, your income and expenditure are not balanced and need immediate attention.

Scrutinizing Income vs. Expenses

It is vital to monitor our income and expenses and keep them in tandem. Any disparity in maintaining their equilibrium will result either in debts that would only be mounting and multiplying gradually. Spendthrift people often spend rashly and later on suffer financial setbacks that are often irreparable. Moreover, strict monitoring and streamlining of income and expenditure is going to render long-term benefits that would be felt in later stages of life.

Here are some genuine and practical tips to monitor our incomes and expenditures thus to make the most of our monetary funds –

Watch where you are Spending

It is a good money managing strategy to know your expenses to the maximum extent. There may be some unforeseen expenses that may rock your budget, but enough scope should be there in your monthly budget to accommodate them. Include all sorts of expenditures you come across in your day to day life starting from your groceries to your evening drinks. When the entire list of expenditure is going to be on paper, you will realize how much money is spent uselessly on frivolous things.

Cut down the Unnecessary Spending
Now once you have complete and comprehensive list of expenses with you, you know where you income would be going. Trust me; you will have an impulsive feeling to cut short many worthless expenses that may deem to you simply useless. And this very is the objective of listing all your expenses. You can also bifurcate them into categories like – important, less important and least important, etc. The idea is to sift the expenses that you can do without.

Do Not Overindulge
If you have good and steady income, it doesn't mean that all has to be spent and splurged. Spare money is to be saved and sorted so they can be used when the need may arise. For example, if the income is 2000 USD, do not make a budget of that whole amount. Save some money aside and do not count that for the purpose of spending.

Spend Wisely
Wise spending can't be learned or implemented in a single day. It is not a procedure, rather a habit that has to be developed over the time. One can't be a wise spender one particular month and then

start splurging the next. Get into a habit of watching your money and then think practical while spending. Wise money management does not lay stress on being a miser or a money-stasher. It teaches how to be a smart spender so that the worth of every penny is derived out. Start in a small way – like cutting the bills of fast food snacks that tend to be heavy on health, as well as pocket. Instead of this, buy lots of fruits and keep them stocked at home. This will benefit your reckless spending as well as your health.

Escalate your income

Smart spenders and savers are always on the lookout of the chances and avenues that would help them in multiplying their income. If you are a school teacher, start taking tuitions in free time. If you are a chef, start taking cooking classes during the weekend. The idea is to augment the inflow of money via multiple streams. A small effort from your side will open many avenues for bettering your income.

Carry Debit/credit card instead of cash

Do not carry the lot of cash in your pocket else you would be spending the lot of it. Though there are people, who tend to spend more when they have their debit or credit cards in their pockets. Just follow a viable routine that would prevent you from spending recklessly.

Ways to Monitor Your Expenses

There are plenty of ideas, tools and applications that can be used for keeping a track of our incomes and expenditures. You just need to have the intention of using these, and they would take care of the rest of the things. Some of them are –

- **Mobile Phone App** – The latest smart phones come with one or the other kinds of applications that help in keeping the record of monthly income and expenditures.
- **Money Box** – Keep a money box handy in your home and use it to store all the receipts and bill that you pay. This will keep clarity of all expenditures. Also, keep in the box a piece of paper that has the record of income.
- **Calculator** – There are specific budgetary calculators that help in maintain the record of expenses.
- **Diary/Note-book** - Maintain a small pocket diary or a notebook in which you can jot whatever you spend. You would know exactly what have you spent on daily, weekly, fortnightly or monthly basis.

Chapter 3- Creating a Customized Budget

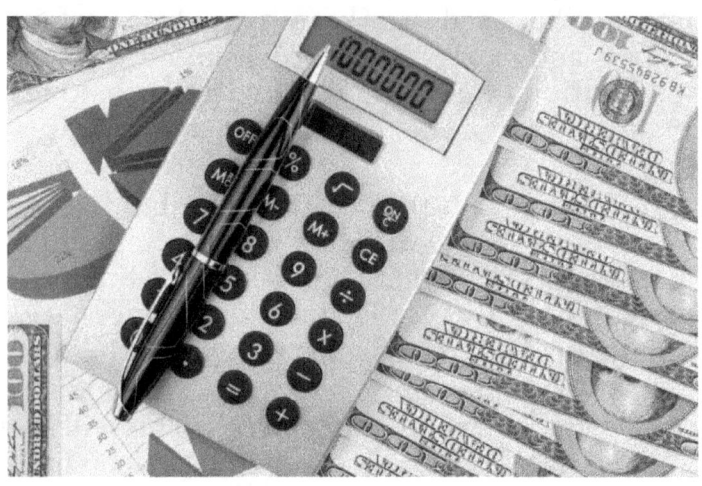

Differentiating between Needs and Wants

The concept of needs and wants must be deeply pondered else money would be spent over futile things. The things we cannot survive without are our needs such as food, shelter and clothing. While these are our basic needs for subsistence, we need many more things during different stages of our life.

Apart from the things that we need to live comfortably, there are few things that we want to fulfill our desires. These are such things that we always desire for but can live without certainly.

Taking the present scenario of life, a family of four can comfortably manage with a two bedroom flat and a mid-segment car. This indeed is their need. However, when they start yearning for a large palatial penthouse and a luxury SUV car, they get trapped in the vicious cycle of wants. The paradox is – Wants never satiate us. Rather, they make us crave even further for bigger homes, latest models of cars and devices, newest brands, etc.

Create a custom Budget that would Fit Needs

A common notion associated with budgeting is that it calls for cost cutting and living with depravities. On the contrary, budgeting helps in maintaining long-term financial health and saves from living in depravation during unforeseen times of financial crises. Learn to create an effective and a practical budget that would perfectly fit your personal needs and requirements.

Have a Simplified Budget

A practical budget is the one that is simple to make, understand as well as apply. Any financial jargon is completely no-no to be included in a budget. Make it realistic and close to your habits and tendencies so that you can stick to it consistently. A simplistic budget would keep you close to your financial resources and would prevent money floundering.

Plan a Long-term Budget

Do not prepare a short-term budget lest you would not be able to purview your monetary savings. The budget should be set for such a period that consistency of results can be felt. A reasonable time span to test a budget should be at least one year. Short term budget would give minimal feelers, and you would not be able to gauge its efficacy. This would include all sorts of inflow and outflow of money including taxes and vacation expenses.

Keep Buffer Funds

While preparing the budget, take into consideration contingency funds so that unforeseen expenses can be taken care of. This fund will also include medical emergencies and make things a lot easier and hassle free. Having buffer funds will come handy in many situations that, if not handled on time, would off-track us financially.

Prepare a Comprehensive and an All-inclusive Budget

A good budget would be the one that would take care of the entire family and their needs collectively. Do not forget any family member starting from young kids and their baby sitting expenditures to elderly grandparents for their medical bills.

Make a Flexible Budget

Don't consider your budget to be a prophetic piece of work. It is good to stick to your budget but be flexible to make some changes and adjustments to get everything running smoothly. Keep ample scope towards its revisions so that no financial crunch is felt on abrupt basis. It is always suggested to bring in some significant changes in the budget rather than waiting it to become a failure and fall flat.

Maintain Effort to Augment your Income/Money Inflow

If your budget is making you live frugally and it is hurting your temperament, make some arrangement to pump in more money in the budget kitty. This way you can have less of cost cutting and enjoy your life comfortably.

Take Pride and Pleasure in following your Budget

Don't pull up a long and a somber face while following your budget. The money you are going to save is going to help you only in the long run. Budgeting isn't a rigorous process that you have to follow with a sad heart. Rather, make it your habit and start enjoying it over the time.

Live within Income and Means

Money needs the wise mind and steady hands for its judicious use. The idea of earning and saving money is to lead a comfortable life where nothing should be wasted. Money should not be spent to impress the world as this is a purely illogical interpretation of happiness. Those who have been leading a financially comfortable life have been living within means, sometimes even below.

Here we give you some tips to live within means and spend your life comfortably ever after –

Understanding the Real Connotations of Being Rich - Different people nurture different perceptions of being rich and wealthy. While some consider having a palatial house and a luxury car a symbol of being rich, others consider having enough for their family's wants, needs with some sensible and regular saving. Though there is nothing wrong in being ambitious and in aspiring to earn all sorts of luxuries, leading a life on the credit or in debts should be the last thing to consider.

Save by means of Sharing - There are many ways to save money in a smarter and an intelligent way. There is one category of people who drive to their work daily alone in their car. There is a kind of person who either takes a tube (despite the fact they can very well afford a car) or form a carpool where colleagues take out their cars turn by turn to commute together. Of course, the second category is smarter in its thinking and remains successful in staying financially stress-free.

Don't Spend Impulsively - Wise spenders have a great control on them and so not shop impulsively. They buy what they need and that too in the way to get the worth of every penny they spend. Don't go to the mall for window shopping. When you need something, go to a proper retail store that is offering quality goods on discounted price. If there is a sale going on trousers, buy them even if you don't need them at that time. Take them out to use whenever you need it later. You would thank yourself for buying it, as emergency shopping is usually very expensive and not worthy.

Don't follow or Trust Advertisements - Do not believe advertisements as they are devised in such way as to make you believe you cannot live without that product. Stay away from them and you would end saving a lot of your money.

Buy only after Comparing - Comparison of price may sap a little bit of your time and effort but will certainly save your money. Comparing the price of things and services will allow saving that would be felt by you. And there are many companies, brands and service providers who dole out wonderful discounts and concessions. So just compare and grab!

Think on larger Perspective - Don't think about saving your money for a short term. Think over a longer time when you would age and would not be able to work and earn as vigorously as now. Invest wisely and start early to reap optimum benefits.

Live Frugally - By staying frugal you would be helping no one else but your own. There is intense consumerism and the world is being driven by that. Do not get tempted to buy latest gadgets, brands and other luxurious items meaninglessly. Buy what you need and only what you can afford.

Stay Healthy for minimal Medical Expenses - Being sick or in some accidental calamity can cause havoc to your finances. Stay healthy and safe to prevent sapping of your savings. Rather invest in your fitness level so that you can enjoy not just good health but also your money.

Avoid being Extravagant - Your friends are going out to eat? Think twice before joining them. Are you going because you haven't been out with them since a long time or just for the heck of it? May be you can avoid it by staying home and saving your money. The objective should be to enjoy without spending senselessly.

Follow Time Management to Manage Money - Many times we have to pay the penalty on bills and invoices for exceeding the last date of payment. This is like abusing time as well as money. So respect your time for better productivity that would further lead to the complete worth of money you spend on various things.

Chapter 4 - Get Rid of Bad Debt

Debts are the most irksome factor that disturbs management of our personal finances. However, debts are not always bad. Interestingly, some of them are good also. The present economic scenario is making it sensible to pay for some of our purchases on credit so that one can make maximum use of their liquid cash. The credit taken will keep the factor of depreciation of money well in control with the help of the rate of interest.

The good debt must never be considered as a liability. It is rather an investment that tends to make our money grow over a longer period, giving us the chance to make optimal use of liquid cash. One apt example of good debt is education loan that is taken to pay for college or higher education. Taking an education loan doesn't always mean that the borrower cannot afford paying the fee in cash. This loan is also taken in order to take advantage of low-interest rate of education loan. Students avoid using the cash of their parents and start repaying their education loan soon after they complete their education and are ready to earn lucrative salaries. A mortgage is also considered to be a good debt as it is considered to be the money saver in the longer run. One can take help of mortgages for buying homes. This kind of debt comes with measly monthly payments while the liquid cash in hand can be used for some other purpose. Good debt is considered to be good for the fact that they come accompanied with the low rate of interest.

In contrast to good debts, bad debts are taken to buy those things or services that lose their worth fast and do not create any promising income in the long term. They also come accompanied with the higher rate of interest. One common example of bad debt is credit card debt that is known for creating a vicious circle of financial liabilities. Buying flashy and branded luxuries through your credit card and then feeling helpless over its non-payment for years to come is a classic example of bad debt. Other types of bad debts are cash advance loan and payday loan that charge astronomical rate of interests that get compounded if not paid on time. These kinds of loans are devised to take advantage of borrower's pathetic and helpless financial condition.

Don't allow accumulation of Bad Debt

Just like a debt can't be accumulated in a single day, it can't be resolved in on a distinct date. The primary requisite to manage our personal finances is to keep away from debts. If you already have few of them to irk you, start planning strategically.

Read below-listed suggestions that would make you wiser and judicious in developing money-saving habits –

Shun debt accumulation

If you are already debt-ridden, just stop there. Do not add more to your already loaded financial burdens. You ought to concentrate over resolving past financial liabilities, thus keep your further track clean and clear. There is no point in clearing one debt by taking two more. This way, your financial status is going to become murkier.

Don't Rely on Credit cards

Credit cards are the biggest reason and cause of bad debts. This financial product gives ready cash to spenders and makes them reckless and mindless spenders. Just keep them away and learn to live without them. Using a credit card simply makes for uncontrolled spending that leads to the further financial mess. Never close the credit card accounts until all debts against it are repaid back lest the credit score will get affected.

Develop sensible attitude

Debt accumulation does not happen out of need but out of lax attitude towards money. This calls for immediate change in attitude so that what causes debt can be cured. A strong will to develop a frugal and a judicious attitude towards money will certainly take care of many financial issues that are known to be caused due to irresponsible mind-set towards.

Alter your spending tendencies

Are you a mindless spender who buys not out of need but out of greed? If you are one such person who cannot restrain buying things that are not even needed, you need to cure yourself. Do not remain lounged in front of TV watching advertisements and ordering things online. Watching online shopping sites just as a hobby is a sure shot recipe for landing in debts. Buying just to look 'cool' in your friend circle will be financially suicidal.

Don't Allow Consumerism to overshadow your lifestyle

Since we live in the times of consumerism, we have started believing that there are many things that are simply indispensable for our subsistence. This is a wrong approach as we are the ones who are responsible for expanding our wants....mistaking them for needs. To ourselves debt-free we must trim our lifestyle and live in a thrifty way.

Add volume to your income

While cost cutting is always suggested for getting rid of debts, opening, and multiple income channels will speed up the process. Better the income, more rapidly you would be able to shrug off your financial responsibilities. And moreover, earning extra is never going to hurt you in anyway. Income can be increased by doing any such thing that interests you. It could be either some money-making hobby of yours (like teaching cooking, music, dance or aerobics) or some skill (being a singer, writer or carpenter, etc.). Having an alternative income channel will cushion your financial crises.

Make timely payments for avoiding penalties

Understand that you are already in debt and paying extra and superfluous charges (that can be certainly avoided) will sap up your resources. Do not delay paying bills, do not jump traffic rules, and do not drive while drunk as these are some of the cases where a lot of money get drained due to sheer negligence and carelessness. Some other ways to save precious money are –

- Withdrawing money from bank instead ATM
- Avoiding online booking of tickets
- Buying credit card after negotiating rate of interest
- Consolidating multiple loans into one single loan that has lower rate of interest

MONEY MANAGEMENT

Making Budget and Abiding by It

Having a budget for your income and expenditure will help in streamlining your finances that are already ailing due to debts. Categorize your expenses and tweak them to fulfill all liabilities as and when required. You will start having a fair idea where and how much to spend, giving you complete control over your money matters.

Chapter 5 - 10 Powerful Money Habits

1. Remain financially aware and educated so that no one can take yours for a ride. You should have a habit of checking and cross-checking your bank details, interest rates, and credit reports. Don't be alien to these important things.

2. Develop acumen to differentiate between need and wants. This will help in having clear financial objectives pertaining to long as well as short-term.

3. Learn to pay close attention to menial yet important details such as your grocery bills, the rates of day to day utilities, and discounted schemes in the offing, etc.

4. Get into a habit of thinking innovative to save your money. It could be like using solar power installer that would save on

your lofty power bills. You can start accumulating shopping points and rewards to redeem them later and get some real worthy stuff. The idea is to develop a habit of saving by being alert, aware and intelligent.

5. One powerful and effective habit is to look for quality and not price. This is a proven fact that quality things are reliable and do not require frequent maintenance that call for the lot of overheads. Buying a cheap pair of shoes over quality (necessarily not branded) shoes is always going to be an unworthy deal as it will soon wear out, and you would have to buy another one soon. This habit finds great relevance especially in buying household utilities and fixtures. In short, the cheaper option may not always be a cost-viable option.

6. Do not feel lazy or lethargic lest you would land up spending lot of superfluous money on frivolous things. Things like ordering from out instead of cooking at home; taking a cab instead of the tube; shopping online instead of visiting brick-and-mortar stores to get some real, worthy deals will sap in lot of money. These things may appear menial but will solidify soon into habits.

7. Always buy for the need and not for the greed. Do not showcase your spending to the world. Buy only for satiating your needs and requirements. Many other important things that would need your finances.

Filtering your needs from wants will go a long way in helping to manage your money well.

8. Develop patience and tolerance in money matters. Getting impulsive in this material-driven world is going to be even more harmful to your money matters. Many times delaying buying of any desirable thing makes us averse to it. So just wait before buying that gold-rimmed spectacles you have been eyeing. You will realize that they are not as worthy as you had thought it to be.

9. The habit of saving, however little, should be developed right since you have started earning. Saving can be a real help in accruing your funds and then investing them for further escalation. Find a good and an effective saving method (saving accounts or fixed deposits) and start keeping some amount consistently without fail.

10. Last but not the least, replacing your credit card with your debit card is one habit that needs to be adopted soon. This will make your realistic towards your finances and not let you spend on impulse. Rather, it is suggested to stop keeping your credit card in your wallet. It should only be used for maintaining your credit record.

Chapter 6 - Investment Guide to Managing Your Money

In recent times, accessibility to financial data and online brokers has made it very easy to invest your money. It is now just as easy as opening a savings account. But in this do-it-yourself world where everything is Internet-driven, can you invest yourself too? If this is true, why don't you pay fewer fees to your mutual funds or even sack your financial advisor and get a portfolio of your own?

Social media and the Internet is not the way it was before, and it has, in turn, revolutionized the way we live. Purchasing stock is harder compared to previous years. You'd have to go through a complex network of specialists and brokers before you could make a single trade. All of that changed in the year 1983 when a Michigan dentist made the first online stock with a system that is similar to what we now call E*TRADE Financial.

Is Managing Your Own Money a Good Idea?

That single trade changed everything about investment products, that is, how they are discussed, researched, bought, and sold. Computerized trading had helped to produce highly liquid markets where you can buy and sell securities easily and quickly. You can now have easy access to the same financial data used by professionals, and websites like StockTwits also have a community of traders and investors that exchange information in real time.

Because it's possible, does that make it a good idea? Specialist investors have a saying "The stock market is the most expensive place to learn how to invest. " they understand that losing money is way easier than making it, and due to this, people have sometimes argued that the vast amount of information available to investors without an experienced financial background is offering a false sense of security.

You can only efficiently utilize the tools you were given if you have the right experience and knowledge. An expensive software package for music won't make any beautiful music without the world's best composers, or will the best innovation in surgical technology make someone without any medical knowledge a world-class surgeon?

Even though the Internet had provided the retail investors with the tools they need to manage their money, they still lack the experience and knowledge to use the tools efficiently. As an investor that wants to manage his money, what are the fundamental knowledge needed to apply tools efficiently?

Modern Portfolio Theory

Understanding the modern portfolio that gives you in-depth knowledge on how asset allocation works for an individual investor based on their factors. You also need to dip deeper than all the high-level Internet articles that define MPT as simple as understanding allocations. MTP is a lot more about efficiency than just an assignment. Most of the best money managers know how to place your money for the best return with the least amount of risk. They also understand that efficiency is very dynamic and the financial picture of a person changes as he/she ages.

Another important thing that comes with efficiency is risk tolerance. Our risk tolerance is liable to change at any point in our life. For example, along with retirement, one might have financial goals like starting a new business, or saving for college, the portfolio must be adjusted to execute these goals. Proprietary software is often used by financial advisors to produce detailed reports that are not readily available to the resulting investor.

Understanding Risk

With the abundance of resources available nowadays, risk is now treated as a trivial matter. "Risk tolerance" is now the prevailing trend among retail investors that they believe they understand risk if they know that they can lose money from time to time. Understanding risk is far much more than that.

Risk is a complex behavior that is sometimes difficult to understand and rationalize because investors act opposite their best interest sometimes. A concise study made by Dalbar Inc has shown that inexperienced investors usually sell low and buy high and this often leads to losses both long-term and short-term.

Risk is a behavior; therefore it is challenging to have an unbiased and accurate picture of investors attitude towards risk. Most day traders that are seen to have a high-risk tolerance can have a low one because they're not willing to hold an investment for an extended period. Professional and successful investors know success only comes when you make decisions based on facts and fend off emotions. This is not an easy thing to do especially when you're working with your money.

Can You Beat the Market?

Do you know the probability of you outperforming the overall market? What is the likelihood of any soccer player being better than most of the other soccer players, and even if they shine for the first year, what is the possibility of them being the best for decades?

Efficient market hypothesis (EMH) is the right answer to your question. This theorem states that all the information about an investment product is factored into the price. If a company like Intel releases information that explains that sales will light this year, the market will immediately adjust and react to the value of the stocks. EMH dictates that prices reflect fair or actual value. Therefore the market cannot be beaten.

Real investors that often randomly select individual stock names with the aim of achieving gains that are even bigger than the whole market would have to wait for a long time since it is just gambling. Although, short-term benefits build over a short period, the proponents of EMH say the market will eventually shut down and the strategy will eventually breakdown.

Even the best of the best when it comes to investment employing teams of researchers around the world were not able to win the markets game over a light period, according to a popular book by Charles Ellis, "Winning the Loser's Game: Timeless Strategies For Successful Investing." Although, critics have jumped on his neck by citing investors like Warren Buffett that has beat the market consistently for a while, how does EMH relates to an individual investor? Before you decide your investing strategy, make sure you have the statistics and knowledge to back it up.

If you're trying to pick stocks with the hope that they'll increase in value faster than the overall market, what are the evidence that backed up your idea? If you plan to invest in stocks for dividends, do you have any evidence to prove the income strategy works? How does investing in index fund works? Where is the right information to make the best decisions?

Learning to Invest
What do you do for a living? If you're part of the majority with a college degree, you might be part of the ones that claim your results did not make you highly skilled, but it was the experience instead. When you started your first job, were you effective in the first place?

You need quite a few experiences before you can manage your own money. You can quickly gain experience from investors but it also constitutes that you lose money, and losing your retirement money is not part of the plan.

The best way to gain experience is by watching the market and learning how it reacts to daily events. Professional investors have discovered that the market is never constant. It can be hypersensitive to news sometimes, and it'll just brush them off some other time. Some stocks have muted reactions while others are highly variable.

Another excellent way for retail investors to gain experience is by setting up a paper or virtual trading account. These accounts will help you gain experience before putting your real money to the markets.

The Bottom Line

The truth is, a lot of people have successfully managed their money, but before you take the risk, make sure you're a student in the art of investing. It is never advisable to do any business based on readings on the Internet. If you're looking to employ a financial advisor, can you consider hiring yourself with your current level of knowledge?

You might be thinking maybe 'Yeah,' but the truth is, until you have the experience and knowledge as a manager, you can't handle a brokerage account with a lot of cash like your retirement money.

CHAPTER 7 - Budgeting: Money Management

Budgeting is not the same as just saving money. It also entails determining where your money goes and taking control of your spending. Research has shown that up to 60% of American households do not have a budget, and up to 11 million adults do not monitor the way they spend on housing, entertainment, and food. When asked, up to 77 million people gave themselves grades ranging from F, and C, to D regarding their knowledge on personal finance. These alarming statistics have shown that there is no better time to start a budget.

A budget is a form of financial plan that compares a person's income with their expenditure to meet personal goals and analyze spending. Since most people need to pay expenses monthly, it is best to create a budget based on monthly income. It is okay to make a yearly budget too if that's what you prefer.

Creating a Budget

Step 1 – Income:

First and foremost, you must figure out the amount of income you're earning. People's income usually comes from their employer, and you won't have a lot of control on this part of your budget. Other sources of revenue include tax refunds, proceeds from a sale, and gifts. Make sure to list all possible sources of income for the next month.

Step 2 – Expenses:

You have more control over this part of your budget since you're the decision maker. Make sure you establish a difference between wants and needs when evaluating your expenses. Although it is okay to buy what you want, you should always prioritize your needs first. Here are some common types of expenses:

Fixed expenses – They are monthly expenses that always have a set amount. These types of expenses make our budget easy because we know what is expected, although, they also make things difficult since we don't have control over them. Examples of fixed expenses include mortgage loans and car payments.

Varied expenses – Varied expenses are the opposite of fixed experience since they change month to month. They are the type of costs we have control over. It is easy to decrease or increase their amount depending on your budgeting needs. Examples of various expenses include utilities, gas, and groceries/food.

Periodic expenses – These are the types of expenses that don't pop up every month, but it still very important to figure them out to ensure you'll be with the money when the need arises. Typical examples of periodic expenses include personal property taxes and create insurance.

Unexpected expenses – As the name implies, these are expenses that we never really prepare for. Motion financial advisors will advise that you spare up to 10% of your budget for this. If you can't save up to 10%, you can start up with less and improve to this percentage. The amount is not necessary, and the goal is to cultivate a saving habit in case of unexpected expenses and emergencies. Example of unexpected expenses includes home repairs, car repairs, and medical bills.

Step 3 – Do the Math:
After you have determined your income and expenses, remove your costs from your income. Some money should be left over. If it doesn't, you

still need to take a closer look at your expenses to cut some costs. Here are some ways to do that.

Ways to Boost Your Budget

Some simple changes in your lifestyle can help cut your expenses by a significant amount in various key categories:

Food

- Clips coupons
- Eat out only on special occasions
- Join a grocery store membership to get automatic discounts
- Skip the
- soda and opt for a glass of water to save up to one-fourth of your total bill
- Make a list to plan your grocery purchases

Clothing

- Sell the clothes you don't need or wear anymore at rummage sales or consignment stores to get back some of its costs
- Shop at thrift and consignment stores
- Look for discounts

Transportation

- Take a bike when the weather allows
- Combine your trips when you run errands
- Use public transport if it's available in your area
- Share rides within your neighbors or co-workers to reduce fuel costs
- Make timely car maintenance to mitigate or eliminate repair costs

Utilities

- Use thermostats that are programmable to adjust your home temperature automatically. Try to set it a few degrees warmer when the air conditioner is on and a bit colder when the furnace is running
- Run the dishwasher or washing machine with as much load as possible
- Make sure you turn things that are not in use off
- Be sure to look for the 'Energy Star' symbol and approval whenever you're buying an appliance to reduce cost on electricity and to also qualify for rebates from power companies. Find out the payback period of these appliances to be sure if you're saving.
- Look for Internet, cable, cell, and telephone bundles that offer to save for multiple services from a vendor.
- Review all the services from cable, internet, wireless companies, and telephones. There's a chance you're paying for a service you don't need.

Entertainment

- Go on faraway travels instead of local vacations. Take advantage of nearby amusement parks, explore regional tourist sites, and visit family
- Go for low-cost craft sessions or meet friends for weekly walks instead of lunch or shopping.

- Cancel one of your smartphone, internet, satellite bill, or cable
- Cancel your subscriptions and read newspapers and magazines instead. You can also share newspapers, books, and magazines with your neighbor or coworkers to reduce costs
- Take advantage of rummage sales for low-cost movies, recreational items, and materials ranging from knitting needles to basketball gloves
- Borrow DVDs, CDs, and books from the library instead of buying them.

Shelter
- Make necessary renovations and repairs yourself. You can easily wallpaper or paint a room yourself
- Try to share your home to reduce expenses. If the room is just too large for you, or an older member is looking for company, that might be your chance. You can also rent your apartment to international students for short term purpose.
- Consider buying the house that you need not your "dream house" or the biggest house
- Consider the type and size of your home that meets your needs, and this includes a condo, single-family residence, condo, or apartment

Miscellaneous

- Save postage online by paying bills. Different credit union provides online bill payment methods that are mostly free.

Increasing Income

Another simple way to reduce your financial problem is to increase your income, although this usually depends on varying factors like family conditions, job skills, economic factors, and others. Even with this, there is a surprising number of ways to increase your income.

Take a second job – To be honest, things can be challenging when you get a new job, but it is not impossible. You'd have to balance things with your household. You can opt for jobs at department stores that give employees a discount on their purchases to help stretch their budget.

Think creatively – Let's take, for example, a family earns extra cash by taking on a paper route to increase their weekend spending allowance. Another earned money by providing a dog sitting service for owners that are on vacation.

Set long-term goals – Although, it might not be possible to increase your income now, making and following a reasonable spending plan will make it possible to fund the pursuit of long-term goals, such as higher education, additional job training, and even relocating to another place.

Sell something – If you can't afford to own any properties of yours, sell it to bring flexibility to your budget and to reduce your debt. If you also have any hobby that people are willing to pay for, consider using it as a source of income. Sell unwanted items in your homes at a yard sale and clean out your house.

Work overtime – Some companies allow their workers to request overtime and also volunteer for assignments that'll increase your income.

CHAPTER 8 - How to Begin A Side Business While Working other Jobs

These times are tough; let's face it. The rate of unemployment keeps increasing, and the cost of gas and food prices are following it up too. People are now looking for ways to supplement their income out of necessity.

People are now able to successfully create a side business while working on their full-time job. But as easy it may seem, it is an excellent bold step that people often seem to underestimate the effort, money, and time it takes.

You should consider starting a side business if you're serious about increasing your monthly income. Although, it is advisable to take a comprehensive guide first before making this move.

Reasons to Start a Side Business

The first and foremost reason to start a business is to bring more money. After all, a side business is a very significant source of making extra income, and you can efficiently run one even if you're working a full-time job. Here are a few reasons to start a side business while maintaining a full-time job.

1. To Save for Something Big

Having a part-time job gives you a chance to save for things you can't afford like a car, swimming pools, vacation, or a house. Their salary will help them pay for their everyday expenses, and the money received from their business will serve as special fund reserved for desired purchases.

2. To Maintain Health Insurance

Having proper health insurance is usually not cheap for self-employed personnel, and it's generally worse for an entrepreneur if there's a family in the picture. People who can't afford the cost of health insurance usually keep their jobs for this particular purpose. Then, if and when their picture becomes successful enough to provide insurance, they become a full-business owner.

3. To Save More for Retirement

Social Security is quite questionable nowadays, and pensions are not as sure as it used to be. Many people have realized their hard work is the only thing that'll wait for them when they can't work anymore. People are now using their side business as a means to secure their future and fund their retirement.

4. To Test a Product or Business Idea

It is usually a terrible idea to leave a stable job to venture out into unknown territory, which is the main reason why people typically inquire about the demand for their new gig while enjoying the benefits of having a full-time salary. The concept is usually best if you have a new and unique idea and you're not sure if the product will do well in your region. Since you're committing to your job full-time, you have a safety net if things don't work out as planned.

5. To Build Cash Flow

Having the appropriate amount of capital can be the critical difference between failure and success. This is why it is quite essential to have a considerable amount of money before you launch your business full-time. The real problem is, people, don't have months of operating expenses that are required to do this. Therefore, people often start with a side business so they'll be able to increase their cash reserves for a full-scale business.

Things to Consider Before Making a Decision

Now that you know the necessary details needed to start a side business, the next important step is to prepare for what's coming. To do this, you need to know what to expect. People often underestimate side businesses and think it won't take much effort. Unfortunately, the reverse is usually the case. A side business usually comes with lots of issues and challenges just like a full-time business. Here are a few things to consider before starting.

1. You'll Have Two Demanding Jobs

You should probably not opt-in for a kind of business that'll require your participation at all time of the day especially if you have a full-time job. For example, if you open a business that will need customers to see you at all times of the day, you'll be limited to lunch breaks only. Also, it is a terrible idea to communicate through email or take phone calls during your full-time job. An ideal side business is the one that'll allow you to dictate your hours. After all, it won't look good in a full-time job is affecting your side business or vice versa.

2. Get Ready for Stress

Let's take this scenario for an example if you're at work and your regular customer from your side business needs help. He might have issues with what you delivered and require you to fix it as soon as possible. If you don't, he won't pay you, and you'd have to suffer the loss. But they, you have a serious project that's due in your full-time job. What will you do?

Every job has a stress factor. Therefore, if you're juggling a side business and a full-time Job, know that it is double the trouble. Although, if you're prepared with the nature of the knowledge and the problems that come with it, you'll be able to deal with it better. Make sure you weigh your priorities before making a tough decision about your business.

3. Don't Be in a Rush

If you're operating a part-time business, you should accept the reality that it won't grow ad fact as a full-time business. A lot of business owners have been discouraged because their business is taking a lot of time to develop. Hypothetically, the growth of a company is directly proportional to the amount of time invested in it. Therefore, if you're putting a few hours plus weekends to your business, it'll take a while before it grows.

The positive part is that you're earning your regular income while investing in your business which may boom at any time. Also, if your side business begins to boom with potential, you can easily quit your full-time job.

4. Say Goodbye to Weekends

A side business will take up a lot of your time even before it grows especially if you're starting and you're setting up your whole system and simultaneously looking for customers. You'll most like be working on your side jobs on the weekends and your main job during the weekdays. This will reduce the time for family and personal relationships. Don't forget your time commitment and other things to consider before you start your business.

How many personal calls will you have to take daily? How many hours do you have to sacrifice daily to communicate with your customers and to develop leads? What about accounting tasks? Do you have to deal with suppliers all the time?

Make a concise and realistic calculation and make sure your lifestyle is compatible with the job. Also make sure that apart from sacrificing your time, you also have your full family support for the business.

5. Be acquainted with the Rules at Your Full-Time Job

Company rules vary when it comes to working other jobs. Make sure you're clear about the rules of your company before you open a side business. Also, if you're creating a competing service or product, there is a high chance that you'll lose your job, especially if there's a non-compete clause in your contract. You could even be subjected to a lawsuit if your product or service is a rub off from your full-time Job.

And most importantly, be careful about the time you use on your side business especially on your full-time job. It won't be polite if your company finds out that you're spending more time on your side business, you can get fired. Try to do most of the work of your side business at your own time. Stay guided.

Analyze Your Business Idea

After you have analyzed the pros and cons of starting a side business, the next important step is to create a business idea. Since it's a side business, don't forget you need a solid plan that'll require little energy and time to invest. Use these four items as a guide for developing your concept.

1. Does It Solve a Problem?

Many successful businesses have a single factor in common nowadays as they have seen a particular problem with which they have provided a solution. This is even more important in this kind of economy where people are looking to purchase things that'll make their lives more comfortable. This is how an idea like cloud storage, plastic diapers, and liquid paper came into being.

This is the path your side business should follow. You don't necessarily need to create something new, although if you're offering an existing service or produce, make sure you provide an equal level of professionalism and function even if it's just a side business.

2. Do You Love the Idea?

Most successful business owners are in love with their business idea. Don't forget, you'll be marketing it, selling it, and you'd have to rant about it all the time. Also, you'll spend a lot of time working on trying business, which means some of your free and family time will go to the business. Therefore, if you don't love the idea, you won't have the endurance and fuel to keep going.

3. Is the Market Broad Enough?

Before you start your side business, make sure you have a broad market that'll help sustain the market. A lot of new business owners mistakenly provide service or product that is only needed by a few, without having a specific target market. This is especially worse when it comes to side businesses. Even if your market has a particular target audience, make sure there enough to keep the market going. Remember that, since it's a side business, you'll need less effort and more customers to keep going.

4. Have You Tested It?
Make sure you test your concept, product or service before putting up the proverbial shingle. The last thing you want is to sell a product that doesn't work, or have a service you're not even prepared for.

If you're looking to provide a form of service for your customers, make sure you do some run-throughs and understand the potential problems and roadblocks that it may develop in the future. If you're looking to sell a product, make sure you have used it for a while so you'll be confident about the quality of what you're selling to people.

Tips To Help You Start Your Side Business While Working Full-Time

After you have passed through all the above and your idea still holds weight, then it is time to plan your daily operations and business launch.

1. Set a Schedule and Goals

One of the best things that will keep your business running smoothly is to get a schedule that maps out your weekly, monthly, and yearly goals, and keeping track of them along the way. Making realistic goals and keeping them on track will give you an edge and keep you on your timeline, which in turn will lead to business success. Although, if you're not thinking of leaving your full-time time job for the side business, create a realistic plan that'll help you stick with both.

Like most new business owners, you'll probably underestimate the amount of time that'll be spent on additional tasks in your side business. Document your time and be organized; this will allow you to keep track of your achievement and the amount it took. If you think the goals that you set are too aggressive and unrealistic, try to be more flexible and change them. If you need additional tips, look for different time management tips that help increase productivity.

2. Get Licenses and Registrations

Get the appropriate insurances, registrations, and licenses in place before you start your side business. Of course, a small business license should be considered.

Do in-depth research about your product or service. Does your business need to be registered and licensed before you start? Get all that you'll need according to the state law of your area. For example, if you're looking to help people with tax, you'll need to be registered, licensed, and bonded in different states, and not just that, you'll sometimes need to carry omissions and error insurance in some countries.

If it's a product that you're looking to offer, you need insurance against faulty accidents or operation caused by the product. Also, if you're a sole proprietor, you are liable to get sued, and your assets will be at stake. Just be sure that you have all the insurance needed and you clearly understand the risk associated with not having them.

3. Set Boundaries

It is very crucial to set boundaries when you're starting a new business if you want to keep your schedule. For instance, if you're looking to work only s day on the weekends, you can spend the rest with your family me members. Just know that you might lose some customers because you won't be able to meet their needs sometimes. Also, after you set your goals, make sure you stick to your guns and don't compromise your priorities.

4. Take Advantage of Your Salary and Set a Budget

Some business can be started without any form of investment, and this is the same for a side business. Make a concise list of your small-business expenses and start-up cost monthly as part of your planning process. Try to find out how he much it'll cost you to start a business and the way to pay for it.

Most people use their salary from full-time jobs to start a business. If you're doing this, make sure the salary covers both your business and personal expenses. Always pay down debt to increase your credit score and also to decrease your monthly expenditure. This will also open credit lines for your business expenses.

5. Play up Your "Weakness"

One of the biggest problem associated with having a side business is that you can read always be available for your clients in this asthma paced world where people need service instantly. But, if you play your games right, this weakness can quickly turn to strength.

For instance, you can make yourself someone that's available when others aren't – usually on weekends, holidays, and after business hours. Make sure your clients are aware of your business hours by listing them in your voice mail, stationery, website, and business cards. If they know you won't be available until after four during the weekdays, they won't be annoyed when it happens.

6. Catch the Big Fish

The best thing to do in most business is to find customers that are ready to give you instant business. You can do this easily by talking to your family and friends about your new venture and also ask them to refer you. It is time to put your networking skills to work.

If you're not a naturally aggressive sales person, you need to get out of your comfort zone if you want your business to succeed. People will reject you sometimes, but if you keep going, you'll get more customers. Remember, some of the most popular and successful entrepreneurs are the ones with the most failures.

7. Consider Your Co-Workers

You will get to a point in your business when you need to outsource. This is even more important in a side business since you'll be working with time constraints. Well, the good thing is, you'll have access to a pool of talents in your co-workers from your side business.

For example, if you need a website, you can easily contact the tech guy from your full-time job. If you need an accountant, you can look for one in the accounting department that need some side income.

However, be sure to explain to them to keep their full-time job and side job separate just the way you do, and that they will work on a contract basis for you. Your agreement should incorporate a Timeline and should always be professional. You should also receive a receipt or a work order at least, the same way you will from any other contractor.

Conclusion

It is way easier to gain money from different streams of income than to earn from a single job in this economy. Just imagine the number of people that lose their jobs daily, the side job serves as a safety net and a good tactic to make more money. Now, if you want to develop it into a full-time business or keep it as a source of extra income, the ball is in your court.

Make sure you have considered the concept thoroughly though, you can test it among friends and family first, and help secure their business too. Hold yourself accountable, be organized, and commit to your plan. Don't forget you're the boss of the company, learn to discipline yourself and commend yourself when the time comes. And lastly, if you fail the first time, don't give up, just keep on trying!

Meenakshi Narang